Items should be returned on or befc
shown below. Items not already rec
borrowers may be renewed in persc
telephone. To renew, please quote

D0129843

5 YEARS TO SAVE THE IRISH CHURCH

First published in 2018 by

columbaBOOKS

23 Merrion Square
Dublin 2, Ireland
www.columbabooks.com

Copyright © 2018 Columba Books

All rights reserved. Without limiting the rights under copyright reserved
alone, no part of this publication may be reproduced, stored in or
introduced into a retrieval system, or transmitted, in any form or by any
means (electronic, mechanical, photocopying, recording or otherwise)
without the prior written permission of both the copyright owner and the
above publisher of the book.

ISBN: 978-1-78218-351-8

Set in Freight Text Pro 11/14
Cover and book design by Alba Esteban | Columba Press

Printed by SprintPrint, Ireland

5YEARS TO SAVE
THE IRISH CHURCH

**TALKS FROM THE NATIONAL
COLUMBA BOOKS CONFERENCE**

MARY MCALEESE

FR MARK PATRICK HEDDERMAN OSB

FR BRIAN D'ARCY

SISTER STAN

FR JOE MCDONALD

---

columba
BOOKS

CONTENTS

INTRODUCTION

Readers may ask 'why five years to save the Irish Church?' And it's a valid question; why not ten years, for as someone else said, "Five Years is far too generous a time frame for the Irish Catholic Church to get its house in order".

The 'five years' simply came about from separate discussions with some of the authors in this book about the state of the Church, and what struck me was that they all felt that a short amount of time was left for the Church to turn things around or else risk just slowly fading into perennial decline and perhaps ultimately disappearing from the lives of the majority of the citizens in this country altogether. Five years was the approximate time span most mentioned.

Certainly many non-Catholics wish the Church would pack up its bags, go and let Ireland be a secular, liberal country where religion is a private matter for the individual, but has no role in education or healthcare. However, Irish Christianity has been around too long to be extinguished so easily. It runs deep in our veins and has had many different peaks and troughs throughout history. What this book is really about is looking at the version of Catholicism that we now see collapsing in Ireland and how even many Catholics feel a strong 'good riddance' towards it. It is a call to those in authority in the Church and to us all, that 'more of the same' will end in tears, and that only a clear vision and radical change to achieve that vision will right the boat of Irish Catholicism. It is a call to arms for the laity because the so-called 'sleeping giant' of the Church is far from awake and ready to take control. It is saying that despite all the scandals and crisis, the Church hasn't spent all its capital, and that there is still a lot of goodwill out there among people whose experience of the Church has been positive, which is often down to the good priest or well-known religious working in their local community for the good of all. Does all this need to be lost before we can find the way forward, or is now the time to say let's stop the rot and find what unites us and build on that as a Church community?

Above all, this radical change will need good leadership – a servant leadership that abandons clericalism and works in a collegial manner.

Five Years to Save the Irish Church is a clarion call from some of the most respected and challenging religious commentators of our time. The reader may not agree with all their views or proposals, but one cannot dismiss their passion for a Church that few now publicly profess to care for, and their extensive experience in working for a better Church and society. We hope that this book fuels a fire of hope and change for the Church in Ireland.

Garry O'Sullivan
MD Columba Books

BIOGRAPHIES

MARY MCALEESE is a former President of Ireland and currently devotes herself to the study of canon law.

FR MARK PATRICK HEDERMAN is a Benedictine monk and former Abbott of Glenstal Abbey in Limerick with a background in education.

FR BRIAN D'ARCY is a Passionist priest and long-time newspaper columnist and broadcaster whose writing focuses on the Gospel in modern-day life.

SR STAN KENNEDY is a social justice campaigner who has founded a number of charities and frequently writes about meditation and spirituality.

FR JOE MCDONALD is a Dublin parish priest with a passion for the life and teachings of Jesus Christ.

LISTEN TO THE PEOPLE

FR BRIAN D'ARCY

I welcome the opportunity to share thoughts, suggestions and reflections with you in this essay. I share these thoughts fully aware that I don't know the future. All I know is that God will always be with us. There will be a future and we will determine it consciously or otherwise. There is no single solution, other than to listen to the Spirit so that God will guide us to the future God wishes us to have.

We won't solve problems right now, or in five years either. We must be more humble than that. It has taken centuries to get us to where we are and the journey will continue with or without us. However, it is our privilege and our duty to reflect upon the crises in the Church we love and it is our duty to admit, humbly, that we're lost, vulnerable and in need of help.

As the Welsh religious poet David Jones observed in *Anathemata*: "It is easy to miss him – the living God – at the turn of a civilisation." We are right in the middle of such a turn. From a Church point of view, the age of Trent is over and done with. That is a great blessing. Why we Church people cannot see that the Church of Trent is a burdensome, outdated model, is beyond me. We've held onto this outdated model for too long.

This is an opportunity to let the Spirit breathe the Church

Leabharlanna Poiblí Chathair Baile Átha Cliath
Dublin City Public Libraries

of Vatican II into existence. What a privileged age to live in.

Inevitably, I may seem to be overly critical. It is not intentional. Rather, it is because I am utterly frustrated at how our Church, which I love, and to which I've dedicated my entire life as a layperson, religious, and as a priest, is failing to listen to its most loyal members. We shouldn't be in this present crisis; it was both predictable and avoidable.

PART I

Some of the most dedicated and gifted people, priests and lay people, walked away from our Church because of the Church's failure to engage in the discernment process so necessary for the transformation we must embark upon. It is a truism to say that what we don't transform, we transmit.

It seems to be a pattern with human institutions. Inevitably, through human weakness, attachment to power and position prevails to the detriment of the mission. 'Deny, delay and defend' is how the malaise is described in secular terms.

Vocations are gifts from God. The shortage of priests is surely God asking us to be different in order to meet the needs of a different world. It is seriously wrong to cling to a model which requires many male celibate priests when we are being led to reach out to the many wonderful gifts of the laity. It is not a problem. It is God asking us to facilitate God's many gifted believers.

In preparation for writing this, I went to Knock Shrine, as is my wont, for a day's reflection.

I became aware that my view of the Church in crisis is distorted by a deep guilt. Here's why. At the beginning of my priestly ministry 49 years ago, the churches were as full as the dance halls I attended nightly. More by accident than design, both became places of ministry for me.

In the dancehalls I got to know ordinary people who were totally at home as they met, chatted, dated and danced. I was the one who was out of my comfort zone, initially at least. I went out of the monastery to discover what the real world was like. They willingly shared their troubles with me, their joys, and their problems. From those generous, honest people I got to know their thoughts and how they lived. I learned they were able to skilfully manipulate the domination of the Church and its clerics. They told them what they wanted to hear but blissfully lived their lives by making their own choices according to their own conscience. The Church in Ireland was a whited sepulchre. We clerics thought the country were solidly Catholic and under control. Yet how could the Church collapse so quickly if it was built on a foundation of faith?

I had to learn that the lay people I met were good people but paid little heed to the rules, regulations, controls or customs of the institutional Church. They played the game when it suited and made their own decisions when it didn't suit. Think *Humanae Vitae*, for example.

Since the early 1970s I have been aware of the growing disillusionment of the people the clerical Church lost touch with. In and around the dancehalls (and a few years later *The Sunday World*) people appreciated that I shared with them the healing Sacrament of Reconciliation in smoky corners of ballrooms. I did it because I believed that Christ would do exactly the same. I did it quietly because I knew the clerical Church would never approve.

In the dancehalls I was enlightened. Faith is not just about what happens in church.

Life has many valid liturgies. Patrick Kavanagh spoke prophetically about the liturgy of the seasons. "O give me faith/ That I may be/ Alive when April's/ Ecstasy/ Dances in every/ Whitethorn tree."

In the Church, on the other hand, I had to be secretive, political, 'safe' and above all, pretend to always be right.

In the dancehalls I found joy and new life from happy people who were shaking off the shackles of oppression. I found the courage to do the same.

In the Church, increasingly I experienced unhealthy attachment to power, control, repression, and whatever the opposite of joy is.

Here's the point: Anything I share with you here I could have told you 35 years ago. It was obvious even then that Church leadership had lost the trust of the people because we abused power and privilege; we made (make?) weapons out of the sacraments to punish and control people instead of inspiring them.

Without wishing to be hurtful, it was obvious that the edifice was built on sand. Religious practice was external and not a living, loving relationship with the person of Jesus our Saviour.

Through the years I've learned that change happens. It can be threatening, but for people of faith it's an opportunity to experience life, religion and Church politics differently. It should be a privilege to embrace each new generation enthusiastically. We should look forward, not backwards. New wine is to be stored in new wineskins. Be courageous about change. It's God's way of keeping us alive.

PART II

The sexual abuse of children by priests and religious is a scandal. However, I believe one of its most destructive qualities was that it gave people, who were already disillusioned with the Church, a legitimate reason to quit.

Here is the real reason for the growing guilt I struggle to come to terms with. On my watch, churches have emptied. We've moved from overflowing congregations to empty buildings; from 90% practice to 9%. We priests have gotten older and more irrelevant; the people have learnt that they can exist more happily without the kind of God, and the largely negative religious practices, we have to offer. We have distorted the saving Word of God. Therefore I have every reason to be consumed by guilt.

I spent my life trying to restructure structures when I should have restructured minds, mostly my own. Faith is not about surviving, it about thriving.

The tragedy is that nowadays so few people appreciate the marvellous gift of the Eucharist, which is the summit and the source of the life of the Church.

This saddens me greatly, yet I know that on those special occasions when people share the Eucharist they find comfort and hope if they are welcomed and cherished.

What does that tell us about those other times when they don't come?

Some years ago, Seamus Heaney was asked to contribute to a book outlining the spiritual lives of influential people. The poet honestly replied that spirituality was one part of his life about which he felt "woefully inarticulate". But to show his goodwill, he included a poem he hoped might be of use. This is part of 'A Found Poem.'

"Like everybody else, I bowed my head / during the consecration of the bread and wine, / lifted my eyes to the raised host and raised chalice / believed (whatever that means) that a change occurred. / I went to the altar rails and received the mystery/on my tongue, returned to my place, shut my eyes fast, made / an act of thanksgiving, opened my eyes and felt / time starting up again."[1]

The Eucharist is "time starting up again". We become what we receive. God is present in the joys and sorrows, forever offering hope and food for the journey.

Yet we know the Eucharist now means so little to so many. How did that happen?

I should be guilty too because I'm not sure many of us have actually learnt the lesson; when we talk about saving the Church we often mean going back to those days of power, control, crowds, pomp and ceremony. We seem to want to return to the outdated times of Trent. That won't happen and it would surely be a disaster beyond words if it did.

PART III

I accept now that I will not be alive to see any of the reforms and changes for which I've longed throughout my entire priestly life, and there's a freedom in accepting it won't happen in my lifetime. It's also vital to admit the need for a different future, even though I don't know what shape the future will take.

---

1   Seamus Heaney, 'A Found Poem', from *The God Factor: Inside the Spiritual Lives of Public People* by Cathleen Falsani, Farrar, Straus & Giroux, 2006.

A better question is: What seed of a living faith will I leave when I'm gone?

However, I am certain of one truism: change will happen. Indeed it has already come in spite of us. The toothpaste is out of the tube and it will not return.

Remember that change is a sure sign of life. Sadly we'll recognise it only when the structures we're so attached to collapse. Transformation seems to happen only when the old falls apart.

As Richard Rohr said, "The pain and the chaos of collapse invite our inner selves to listen at a deeper level and to move to a new place."

Reformation is happening in a positive way whether we know/like it or not. The changes are not from the top down but from the bottom up. Not from the outside in but from the inside out.

Donal Harrington in his book *Tomorrow's Parish: a vison and a path* uses the example of the journey from Dublin to Cork without having to stop at a traffic light. A few years ago, it was Naas, Newbridge, Kildare, Portlaoise, Cashel, Fermoy etc. The towns are bypassed so that we forget they're there at all and only visit them in an emergency or for an occasional break. So it is with the Church: we're by-passed; our services are used sporadically at best now.

PART IV

Our major sin was, and is, putting the maintenance of the institution before the gift of new life offered by the Holy Spirit. We already have form in this matter – didn't we protect the institution and abandon children to abusive predators?

You've often heard it said that if you want to make God laugh, tell him your plans for the future. So here goes.

I was reading some of what I wrote over the years on this topic in preparation for this essay. I found an article I wrote in March 2013 just after Benedict retired and the cardinals were gathering in Rome to elect a new Pope.

I was at my lowest ebb. I was on the verge of excommunication from the Church, though few realised that. I was quite ill and in fact was hospitalised on that day. Yet when Pope Benedict resigned, it was as if the Holy Spirit was allowed back into the Church.

I outlined for *The Sunday World* readers, before the election, the kind of Pope we desperately needed. I wrote, "We need a Pope who will allow us to believe in a God of compassion; a God of the second and third chance; a God of surprises; a God whose love knows no limits, especially for the imperfect, the struggling and the marginalised...

"The new Pope must have the ability and the power to reform and reorganise not only the Curia but the way the Church is governed... Most of all, the new Pope will need to reinstate the practice of collegiality because to fan the flame of collegiality would instantly involve people of talent in the decision making of the Church, especially women. The new Pope must welcome women as full members of the Catholic Church."

Pope Francis was elected five years ago. Like all of us, he hasn't been perfect, but I can assure you that had he not been elected I would not be writing to you now, because I would no still be a priest.

The kind of Church that Pope Francis struggles to create is the only credible plan available to us. Francis emphasises God's mercy. He not only talks, but acts like Jesus, by showing love for the poor and by continually striving to overcome opposition from within. He uses the vocabulary of the ordinary people and communicates as if he's one of us.

He reassures us in *The Joy of the Gospel*, saying, "Everyone can share in some way in the life of the Church; everyone can be part of the community; nor should the doors of the sacraments be closed for simply any reason.

"Frequently we act as arbiters of grace rather than its facilitators. But the Church is not a toll house; it is the house of the Father where there is a place for everyone with all their problems."

His ecclesiology is summed up in simple words and in simple phrases.

His vision is a real vision. To quote again from *The Joy of the Gospel*, "The Church has the responsibility to proclaim the Gospel in ways that pertain to the whole people of God....a preacher needs to keep his ear close to the people and to discover what it is that the faithful need to hear. A preacher has to contemplate the Word, but he also has to contemplate his people. He needs to be able to link the messages of the Gospel to an experience which cries out for the light of God's Word."

That's a faith community he's talking about, not a clerical institution. It's a caring, welcoming, listening, praying and compassionate community.

Francis understands radical change necessarily means dealing with conflict. "It is the willingness to face conflict head-on, to resolve it and make it a link in the chain of a new process." Conflict is positive and to be embraced, not avoided, as we learned from the Acts of the Apostles.

PART V

I realise how irrelevant the clerical Church has become when we try to impose a visionless structure on God's people. I feel lucky in that I've been in a position to listen to the faithful. They trust me enough to share their troubles and their visions every week. In 50 years of broadcasting and over 50 years in journalism I've had a unique opportunity to listen and learn.

The sacraments are where the people should meet a loving God. Yet too often we impose rules and regulations on grieving people because we'd rather be safe than helpful. We make marriages as loveless as our own lives often are. We reduce a person's life to make it fit our little worlds. No wonder people increasingly arrange weddings and funerals outside churches and away from their restrictions.

The growing secularisation in Ireland is a result of many things, including clerical child sexual abuse, an intolerance of dissenting voices, an inability to understand the God-given beauty of sexuality and gender. These are areas where we need to be courageous in order to be relevant.

The Catholic Church is no longer held in esteem by most of the population because when the people meet the Church, too often they experience canon law rather than the law of the Gospel, the law of love.

In short, for better or worse, people don't trust us. When trust is broken it can never be restored. It demands a new relationship altogether, not a patched-up version of what has failed.

If we are to read Pope Francis correctly, we must understand that the core value of his ecclesiology is the creation of a synodic Church. It will be a genuinely inclusive process where there will be free and open debate and consultation. That's the opposite of dictatorship and hierarchy.

Pope Francis is not afraid to make statements, some of which turn out to be controversial. He engages in genuine dialogue. The emergence of a Synodal Church will take time. It will mean the destruction of many of the structures which block progress, including the Roman Curia itself.

There will be a new paradigm of collegiality. It will mean the voice of the faithful and that of all baptised share in the priestly, prophetic and kingly office of Jesus Christ.

PART VI

The Joy of the Gospel, requires all, particularly bishops, to be attentive to the signs of the times so that: "Bishops will sometimes be ahead of their flock. Sometimes walking alongside, sometimes following along behind, and all the time consulting and listening not least to those who tell them things they may not want to hear."

On a practical level I have come to accept that those who believe in the Spirit and the need to change cannot always wait on permission to do things differently. That's the lesson I've learnt from the people I work with, and from praying the Scriptures.

Already the people of God are working out their own relationship with God. They are organising their marriages and their funerals in a way that is meaningful to them, even though what they do is often condemned by the Church authorities.

We must learn from the people. They have discerned that what we offer is not life-giving. They don't have everything right, but they are making a genuine attempt to celebrate their own beautiful lives and to acknowledge the working of the Holy Spirit within their own life experiences.

And that is why one of the most helpful gifts we have to offer is the gift of genuine, non-judgemental listening. By listening, I mean listening not to come up with answers or to correct people, but listening so that we might learn what it is like to live through and celebrate real experiences.

Listening, though, is merely the first step to actually hearing. Change comes only with hearing. And when we actually hear the cry of the poor, we might be moved to respect their life experiences as genuine religious experiences in themselves – and something infinitely more valuable than what we offer them.

To put it simply: what we're doing now is not working. Furthermore, it's not going to work. We are not coming up with solutions because we don't understand the problem. The Holy Spirit is challenging us to let go of what is killing the Spirit and to do what is necessary to involve the whole community in discovering the hidden gifts which will shape a new way of being Church.

I'm not saying we must throw everything out. But what I am saying is that if we continue to insist on imposing our way of being Church, the people will continue to do what they're already doing: walk away. They are telling us that they would rather concentrate on community than on parish boundaries which too often have become a source of power and control.

We need to listen so that we can discover that we have no shortage of vocations, just a shortage of male celibates.

We need to be courageous enough to tell those in authority that the reasons they offer us for forbidding the introduction of women to the priesthood are simply not good enough. We are not simpletons.

I concede there may well be good reasons why women cannot be ordained, but I haven't heard many convincing reasons to date. The excuses we receive from on high today are actually insulting. We desperately need to have a deeper conversation to discover and discern what the truth is concerning the ordination of women to the priesthood as well as the cherishing of womanhood in the Church as is happening daily in wider society.

Women are second-class citizens in the Catholic Church. This is the major issue that must be tackled honestly, not in the future, but now.

Nor is there any obvious reason why married clergymen could not be part of the ministry immediately. (Perhaps a look at the Lobinger Model of Teampriests could be the basis of a workable plan).

Yet the truth is that in the future, the Church will not be a clerically-led Church at all – by men or women. It will grow from the ground up, not hierarchically from the top down.

To conclude: if we're looking for a model for a Church forever in need of reform, we will find it in St Matthew's Gospel in the Beatitudes. The Sermon on the Mount is the blueprint for Christian living and is the heart of Jesus' teaching. It's the heart of the Gospel message.

The alternative reign of God, which Jesus teaches, overturns trust in power, possessions and personal prestige. To be changed by God's words in the Sermon on the Mount we need to have humble, open hearts.

Look at the way Jesus sets the stage for the Sermon on the Mount. He sees crowds following him and heads to the mountain which itself is symbolic, pointing to the new law fulfilling the Mosaic Law.

He begins with a simple message which is the key to everything else: "Blessed or happy are the poor in spirit; the Kingdom of Heaven is theirs."(Matthew 5:3). What does it mean to be poor in spirit? It means an inner emptiness and humility. It is to be able to live without the need for personal righteousness and reputation. It's the powerlessness that is often framed in the first step of Alcoholics Anonymous. It is Jesus saying: Happy are you, you are the freest of all.

Most important of all, Jesus uses the present tense. "The Kingdom of God is theirs." He does not say 'will be theirs'. God's reign is now and not later.

Blessed are the merciful, for they shall have mercy shown them. The experience of mercy and forgiveness is where we meet a God who loves gratuitously. One cannot buy God by worthiness, achievement or obeying commandments. (And if you have time perhaps you could read Psalm 136 to discover the God of faithful mercy). Mercy is who God is. Mercy is what pleases me, not sacrifice. (Matthew 9:13; 12:7)

The mystery of forgiveness is God's entry into powerlessness. Withholding forgiveness is holding onto a form of power over another. It's a way to manipulate and shame and control and diminish another.

Blessed are the gentle. To live simply is to live gently. To live gently in the Church is to be able to let go of an old model so that future generations can experience the beauty of God's presence in our midst. It's to recognise, as all the great saints have recognised, that after a while possessions are what possess us.

The Beatitudes tell us that we must hunger and thirst for justice and, as Martin Luther King Jr put it, "Injustice anywhere is a threat to justice everywhere."

PART VII

Love is the foundation of it all. Jesus did not say: "Thou shalt be right." Jesus said, "This is my commandment; love one another." God's love is planted inside each of us as the Holy Spirit. Love is who we are. Richard Rohr wrote in *The Bottom Up*: "Only God in you can know God...you cannot know or love God with your mind alone."

Love is our foundation and our destiny.

PART VIII

Finally, I believe that we need to be aware of and affirm the genuine prophets in our midst. It has been said that a prophet is one who keeps God free for people and who keeps people free for God.

Could the biggest sin of our modern Church be that we have made God unreachable, unlovable? Somebody wrote recently that, "Too many people have been shamed and taught guilt to keep us clergy in business".

Could it be that the sin of the Clerical Club is to make God less accessible instead of more so? Prophets have the courage to speak the challenging word; they understand where the signs of the times are asking us to go; prophets trust God to remain faithful.

Have we ever thought of what we're doing to people when we

say you can come to God only through us, by doing the right rituals, obeying the rules and believing in the right doctrines? Do we not realise that this is telling God who God is allowed to love?

The surprise of the Gospel is that God continually breaks the approved rules of God by forgiving sinners, choosing the outsider and the weak and showing up in secular places.

In short, our job in the Church today is to spend our lives loving others the way God loves us. But first we must contemplate how God loves us.

The Church of the future will enable us to 'care' for the precious gift of faith by walking a prudent path that protects us from the twin evils of indifference on the one hand and of fundamentalism on the other.

In my own spiritual life I spend more time fearing and trying to control God than actually loving God. The truth is the very opposite. In Jesus God becomes powerless. Seeing God in the form of a small baby indicates the shift of emphasis from power to powerlessness as no other story does, with the possible exception of seeing God nailed to a tree.

Tielhard de Chardin and others, including Henri Nouwen, have told us, "You don't think your way into a new kind of living. You live your way into a new kind of thinking." We need to be courageous and live out the hope we are called to give.

In the 2nd century Saint Irenaeus preached: "The glory of God is a human being fully alive." We are an Easter People, free and fully alive. These are difficult times, but I believe strongly that "things turn out best for those who make the best of the way things turn out", as John Wooden said.

Pope Francis says that "Hope is the humblest of virtues,

because it hides itself in this life." It is a gift from God, he adds, and we must ask for it.

Vaclav Havel says, "Hope is not the conviction that something will turn out well, but the certainty that something makes sense regardless of how it turns out."

For 40 years I helped organise an annual Novena of Hope; The Graan monastery in Enniskillen became famous for The Novena of Hope in a broken community. I'm not pretending that novenas are the answer to dwindling church attendance. As I've said above, the malaise is much deeper than.

However, as an example, the novena grew over 25 years. The speakers were largely lay people sharing their hope-filled stories. All religions came to the Novena, young, old, sick and well. For 10 years at least, the church was overflowing two and three times a day - about 3,000 a day, in the heart of rural Fermanagh. It was a celebration of the joy of being human.

On the last night, we had to ask the PSNI to block the roads half an hour before the service began and to turn away the hundreds we could not cater for.

There aren't many occasions today when we have to police people away from our churches. Such is the power of hope in dark times.

Karl Rahner wisely reminded us that "the number one cause of atheism is Christians. Those who proclaim Him with their mouths and deny Him with their actions is what an unbelieving world finds unbelievable...In the days ahead, you will either be a mystic (one who has experienced God for real) or nothing at all."

That's the challenge facing us in the Church not only in Ireland, but throughout a sceptical world.

CHURCH: CANCER AND CURE

FR JOE MCDONALD

When death gets into the bones, it can progress with a chilling relentlessness, and death has gotten into the bones of the Irish Church. In my opinion, we certainly do not have five years to save the Irish Church. Some aspects of the Church are already dead and others are dying whilst we speak. Therefore, the issue is not whether we are dying, but rather is the death of the Irish Church inevitable? Is it too late, or can we stem the dying?

Are there steps even at this late stage that may stall or indeed arrest this dying? Of course, I am not speaking of the natural dying process that is part of the cycle of life. I am not speaking of the process of rejuvenation that requires the seed to die, but rather I speak of a death that could be avoided. In fact I speak of a death that we are responsible for.

I have noticed that when we begin to speak of a dying or dead Church, some people are immediately compelled to jump to its defense and to frantically speak of the bits of the Church that are still alive. To me, this is a bit like admiring a terminally ill patient's beautiful skin, or worse still, going in to see Granny laid out and admiring her lovely hair.

Some people believe that if you dare to speak about a dying church, you are showing a lack of love for the Church. Yet, in the most intense of relationships, when one is dying, surely it is healthy to speak of the impending reality of death? When this real and painful exchange takes place, there is certainly no diminishment of love. I do accept of course that there are signs of life, of good things in the Church. Indeed, even in recent months there have been some examples of good leadership from a small number of bishops.

Speaking of a dying or dead Church can also lead to accusations of treachery or disloyalty. I resent these charges. I love the Church with a burning passion. It has been said to me, "if you don't like it you should leave." I have no intention of leaving the Church, but I refuse to stand idly watching as the Church that I love chokes and convulses to an early death.

In the recent 1916 commemorations there was much talk of the spirit of the nation. We began to ask ourselves, what is our heritage? What does it mean to be Irish? My reflection and prayer in preparation for this essay has also had me musing on the soul of the Irish Church. I fear that we may be losing the soul of our country, and once it is gone, I wonder how we will get it back.

As a way of exploring the rather challenging premise of this book, I have identified a number of serious ills affecting the Church. I propose to share just four of these with you in this essay. In addition to sharing these four ills I will also sketch something of my vision for dealing with them. The four serious ailments that afflict the Irish Church at the moment can be grouped under the following headings:

1. THE OSTRICH CHURCH

As is pretty obvious in the title, the Ostrich Church refers to the Church's issues with denial and its tendency to bury its head in the sand. The Church has been denying the issues associated with clerical priesthood, or, rather, denying the death of it. Fewer and fewer men are hearing the call to priesthood, and with the dwindling numbers comes the slow but certain death of this long honoured tradition that Jesus founded. Mark 3:13-15 says: "[Jesus] now went up into the hills and summoned those he wanted. So they came to him and he appointed twelve; they were to be his companions and to be sent out to preach with power to cast out devils."

I believe God is still calling women and men to serve him in spreading the Kingdom of God, but we are making a mess of these invitations. So, we ask ourselves: Is it 'que sera sera', or are we prepared to be active co-workers with and in the Spirit, helping to revitalise the spiritual companions in the Church?

We must also look to how this death of the clerical priesthood has occurred. It occurs because of denial as well as genuine blindness, because of apathy as well as complacency. Could it be that the Church itself, as an institution, is guilty of the great sin of pride, and this sin has led to the death of one of its foundational structures?

PROPOSED ACTION

Have the courage to close the seminaries and suspend the present form of vocations.

During this period of suspension, we will have the opportunity to begin identifying and training priests in parishes who are willing to mentor incoming trainees.

We can also begin replacing the old seminary model of formation, creating a new model that emphasises companionship with Jesus prior to the beginning of service and study.

Hand out P45s for the majority of the diocesan vocations directors.

Appoint a committed Catholic laywoman in each diocese to nurture and nourish women and men who are excited about reform and renewal of Church in Ireland.

This Catholic lay woman will lead a small team which will include a priest, permanent deacon, a religious and other women and men to recruit others to help reform and renew the Church.

Draft a new country-wide mission statement for the Church. Ideally this should happen at the Episcopal Conference. This mission statement will help enforce the reform and renewal of the Church that the bishop's have thus far been unable to inspire. The mission statement will clearly state the need to put aside all clericalism, all careerism and all self-interest. The drafting of this mission statement could be followed by a national week of contrition, declaring a commitment to a new beginning that honestly recognises the state of the Church and accepts the need to spearhead reform and renewal.

Encourage bishops to engage in a period of self-reflection,

asking themselves what their involvement in the Church truly is, and whether they are truly committed to the Church and its followers.

2. THE ROLLOVER CHURCH

In many ways we are a battered, beleaguered Church. We have brought some of this on ourselves, and much of it is deserved. Like Zechariah in Luke 1:20-22 and 59-66, we have lost our voice: "Listen since you have not believed my words, which will come true at the appointed time, you will be silenced and have no power of speech until this has happened."

He lost his voice. His voice was restored when he recommitted himself to God's will. We must follow suit, but we are paralysed by fear. Some of it is political correctness, much of it is fear of rebuke.

Often mealy-mouthed, we slide towards apologising for our own existence.

Perhaps the worst example of this tendency to roll over is evident in what we are allowing to happen to the sacred. Just like the trampling of the pearls by the swine, we increasingly witness a trampling of the sacred.

Let me give you an example of what I call a 'trampling of the sacred'.

It's First Holy Communion. The children have rehearsed and practiced for weeks. The teachers and classroom assistants have worked tirelessly. Many parents, at least at some level, recognise this day is a special day. Yet throughout the ceremony a significant group of adults talk—but this is not just passing the odd word to each other. They talk constantly. What

I really cannot get my head around is that they talk during the children's singing, the children's readings and prayers, all of which they have practiced so much and are so eager to do, and to do well. This is not just bad manners; this is not covered by the word disrespect. Rather, this is a 'trampling of the sacred'. We are the only major faith that tolerates growing disrespect in the sacred place reserved for worship. It would not happen in the synagogue, nor should it. Are you seriously telling me our Muslim sisters and brothers would put up with this reprehensible behavior in the mosque? Of course not. Nor should they. Let us not point the finger but rather look in the mirror. We facilitate this pagan trampling. When are we going to shout 'stop'?

Let me also say a few words on another 'trampling of the sacred': our celebration of the Eucharist. To what degree might it be better referred to as the Lethargic and/or the Languishing Eucharist?

There seems to be a wide range of experiences of Mass. This will always be the case and perhaps that's not a totally bad thing. However, should there not be a minimum standard, an acceptable quality of celebration of the Eucharist below which we should not go?

I believe we as priests would benefit from some retraining, from some accountability.

Recently, a priest who is known for a very fast Mass detected in me a bit of unease with his speed in the liturgy, and he somewhat defensively challenged me to name what prayer or part of the Mass he had left out. I readily agreed, "True Pat, (not his real name), true you left out no prayer, nor did you leave out any part of the Mass, but what you may well have left out is reverence."

—PROPOSED ACTION———————————————

Enforce a country-wide liturgical audit by a team of retired Catholic teachers, both women and men, who will evaluate priests on their ability to deliver Mass, asking questions like: Was there any sacred silence? Did the priest read his homily? Was the sacred music prayer or performance? This audit will necessitate the development of an evaluation sheet or template.

Draft a code of behaviour for both priests and congregation giving and attending Mass, emphasising that actions like chewing gum, drinking, putting on makeup and allowing children to run around the church will be not permitted.

Emphasise the idea of sacred silence in the Church. We need to be reminded of the sacred nature of both the place and the action of the Church. What are we doing about the killing of silence? Even some of our monasteries have sold us a little short on sacred silence. Lord preserve us from the gossipy monk, and I am not referring to the guest master! Are we becoming increasingly immune to the desecration of the sacred in front of us? Without becoming technophobic, what are we saying about the advancing tyranny of technology, especially the damage being done by unbridled social media? Adressing the rapid advance of technology will form a key part of the overall programme of reform and renewal that is urgently needed.

End the practice of giving Holy Communion to little children who have little or no understanding of what is involved, the vast majority of whom have no religious support at home. When the day that the child receives his or her Holy Communion for the first time is also the day when that same child receives Holy Communion for the last time, there is something seriously wrong. Parents should be able to chose a day between Holy Communion Day and Graduation Day from primary school for their child to receive Holy Communion, in order to better equip children with the knowledge and respect needed to make this commitment to the Church.

End the practice of Confirming children and instead invite young adults in transition year to opt for this beautiful sacrament then, when they are older and better able to understand and respect the sacrament and the Church as a whole.

3. THE SALTLESS CHURCH

Matthew 5:13 says, "you are the salt of the Earth, but if the salt has lost its flavour, with what will it be salted?" This is a good question. We must consider how much we worry about popularity and political correctness, and ask ourselves whether we should be less worried about a phone call to the bishop and more concerned that somebody will talk to Joe Duffy on *Liveline* next week.

Though this disease of self-awareness and self-absorption is evident, recently I have been encouraged by the leadership of some of the newer bishops. But we must continue their work. We must speak openly about difficult topics like homelessness, exorbitant rent, the increase in violence, domestic abuse, the increasing pervasiveness of suicide, the gradual overall erosion of mental health and the blight of direct provision centres.

I genuinely believe that we, here in Ireland, are sliding into a period of great spiritual darkness, a period where our humility, the very salt of the Church, is being lost.

PROPOSED ACTION

Find our voice as Church and maintain it. Strange as it may seem for me to say, within this slide into darkness, as it gains momentum, and indeed as a direct consequence of it, I actually believe Ireland has rarely needed the Church more. I say this knowing full well that many would argue against such a concept.

However, I would like to qualify how I believe Ireland needs the Church in these days of accelerating secularism.

The glaring need for us as a faith community to find a new place in this secular world will not be satisfied by us as Church triumphant, or Church all powerful, but rather as a Church that finds its voice afresh within the encircling gloom, and dares to passionately preach Christ as the light.

The following words by St. John should not only act as our breastplate and comfort, but also form the backdrop for our preaching: 'The Light shines in the darkness and the darkness can never extinguish it." (Jn 1:5)

Start a conversation about whether faith should be involved in public life. Whilst I am not totally convinced of the *bona fides* of French President, Emmanuel Macron's call to Catholics to become involved in public life in France, a country that has a strict separation of the Republic from religion, is a good one, and one that I think we need to emulate. I was intrigued at the conversation it opened up or rather reopened. In fact, where France is at the moment, for example, on the cusp of decriminalising euthanasia, is where I believe we will be in a very short time.

In Ireland, Catholics who become involved in public life, quickly push their faith to one side. One wonders how much of this is driven by the desire to keep their seat at the next election and raw ambition. Whilst the price will vary, it is a danger for all of us that we will sell our soul to the devil for popularity, gain, or both. This is no less serious when it is done in public office.

I wonder, did any bishop or indeed parish priest contact any member of the Cabinet to discuss not only their life in faith, but also their role in giving example to others? So with this in mind is it even acceptable to ask, can you leave your faith at the Cabinet door, or the gates of Leinster House? Should you? We must seriously consider these questions.

4. THE HEMORRHAGING CHURCH

In Mark 5:25-34, a story is told of a woman who was bleeding for 12 years. The scripture says, "She had suffered a great deal under the care of many doctors and had spent all that she had, yet instead of getting better she grew worse. When she heard about Jesus, she came up behind him in the crowd and touched his cloak, because she thought, 'If I just touch his clothes I will be healed'. Immediately her bleeding stopped and she felt in her body that she was freed from her suffering."

The Church is like this woman, but instead of having internal damage inflicted upon it, its own hemorrhaging is the result of its own actions, its own dysfunction.

We have begun to alienate groups from the Church, including former religious/ priests, the LGBT community, and women generally. And of course we must not forget others who dare to question, who dare to differ.

When asking ourselves if we, by whom I mean us religious

people, have been good models of forgiveness and compassion, the answer is most certainly no.

When asking ourselves how we would treat a new prophet in this age, the answer is: poorly. Just as we treat other so-called 'dissidents', so we would treat a prophet. Maybe there is a clue here as to why we have so few prophets or prophetesses.

There is great division within the Church. Will we within the Church rip each other apart? Very likely. Why? Because we confuse unity with uniformity, but this creeping disunity is doing untold damage to the Church. So-called Catholics who claim on one hand to be faithful but on the other hand have no problem disrespecting and undermining the Pope are undermining the Church. Indeed, we have more than our own share of religious extremists.

The Church is being called to get on her knees and she is having difficulty getting down.

Prayer, humility and service: these are three key ingredients that produce Gospel Joy, and they are the three we must reintroduce to stop the hemorrhaging of our Church.

PROPOSED ACTION

Initiate a period of healing reconciliation with a clear declaration of moving on/doing things differently. The key words in this plan of action include: inclusion, empowerment and declericalisation.

Determine a model or stance of Church to cultivate. Let's develop a model of being Church that is less defensive, and decide whether our power is that important to us. When creating this model, ensure that we do not put those who dare to question, and I might add, dare to question in love, beyond the wall. After all, in these days when we have observed the North Korean Kim Jong-un and President Moon of South Korea walk across the barren desert of no man's land and shake hands, then surely in preparation for the arrival of this great reforming Pope, we could find a way of leaving aside any small mindedness, or meanness of spirit, and graciously accept all, and reach out to those priests who have found themselves under sanction.

An example of a new kind of church is the Parish of St. John XXIII. It is under female management, and these women have complete responsibility for running the parish. Holy Communion is given in the final year of primary school, as requested by parents, and Confirmation is done for students in transition year, again, as requested.

This parish also invites priests on the panel to celebrate the sacraments, and these priests engage in semi-communal living, where they have their own private space, living room, office and bedroom but maintain a communal relationship with other religious.

CONCLUSION

The Secular Age has taken hold in Ireland and we as Church need to get busy preparing for our new role as a minority faith community. Time is not on our side. Our action, or inaction, in these days will have a direct bearing on whether in tomorrow's Ireland, we emerge as a radical witness to the Gospel, or, as is a very real possibility, we become an irrelevant, if quaint, relic of the past. I believe both dust and rust abound in the Irish

Church. Make no mistake, the dust is gathering and the rust is eating away. We must act now to save the Church.

CHALLENGING THE CHURCH TO COMPASSION

SISTER STAN

The Church that Jesus founded was nothing less than the Kingdom of Heaven on Earth, and that was how the early Christians understood it and sought to live it. They understood that we come into the world with nothing and we leave the world with nothing, and nothing belongs to us. In order to live as the Kingdom of Heaven on Earth, the early Christian community was committed to living in radical solidarity, sharing everything they had.

The radical Church that grew up after the Resurrection is the Church that we, as today's Christians, are still called to, but that is not the kind of Church we have today. Jesus lived among the poor, but many see today's Church as being far removed from the poor. There is a fall-off in church attendance and religious practice in general, but it is far more marked in poor areas. The Church in general, which was founded on the principle of solidarity with the poor, is failing the poor.

Instead of being seen as a Church of the poor, and a Church of compassion, today's official Church is seen by most people (and actually is) a Church that is almost entirely focused on its own laws, rules and regulations, laws that have led to the

Church excluding so many people who, as the Church sees it, fall short of these laws: gay people, divorced people, people living in unmarried relationships, priests who speak out against unjust structures in the Church, women who wish to have a much more active role in Church ministry.

Of course there are compassionate people within the Church, but I'm speaking about how it is seen and perceived and experienced by most people. Our Church has long been a structure held together by rules and regulations. Adherence to the laws laid down by the Church has been the defining characteristic of Roman Catholicism. A good Roman Catholic is one who does not get divorced, who does not use artificial means of birth control and who goes to Mass every Sunday.

Adherence to the Church's rules and regulations may well define a good Roman Catholic – but it does not define a good Christian. That is a distinction that today's Roman Catholic Church needs to face up to. A good Christian lives by different rules. A good Christian lives according to criteria laid down by Jesus himself: "By this shall all men know that you are my disciples, by your love for one another." So we have it on the authority of the founder of our faith himself: our defining characteristic as Christians is not our adherence to canon law or the rules of the Church, but rather our love for one another.

Of course laws are necessary, but as Tony De Mello says, "if we concentrate on the laws we can miss the point." He uses the image of a beautiful sunset to explain our relationship to Church law. We see the sunset and point to it, but if we focus too much on the act of pointing to the sunset we miss the sunset itself. Church law is like the pointing finger. The laws are telling us ways of expressing our love for God and one another, but if we concentrate on the laws we miss the whole point. Laws crystallise values, but if we emphasise the laws we are in danger of missing the values that the laws are intended to express.

A Church that places too much emphasis on its own laws not only fails people who cannot live according to those Church-made laws, but it is misrepresenting the nature of our relationship with God. It is putting forward the idea of a God who is concerned with observance of the law, a God whose primary role is as a judge. This is a God that will reward us if we do what we are supposed to do according to the law, and who will punish us if we do not keep the laws. But this is not the God that the New Testament has revealed to us.

By being so concerned with laws and observance of laws, the Church has travelled down the same cul-de-sac that the religious leaders at the time of Jesus travelled. Jesus criticised the religion that over-emphasised obedience to laws. He challenged the Pharisees' idea of a God who is concerned with the law and put forward the idea of a God that is passionate about love and compassion. His followers therefore are to be recognised not as observers of law but as people who are passionate about compassion.

Some of the reasons for these changes in the way the Church thinks and acts are historical. In order to counteract the teachings of Arianism around the year 300, for example, the Church developed a heavy emphasis on the divinity of Jesus, and the Eucharist developed into a ritual of adoration and worship and a means of personal sanctification. But that was not how the early Christians saw the Eucharist. At the Last Supper, when Jesus said, "This is my body, this is my blood", he did not invite the disciples to worship him. What he said was, "This is my body, which will be given up for you. This is my blood which will be poured out for you" and he invited the disciples not to worship him but to follow him.

What we are re-enacting in the Eucharist is this act of self-sacrifice, whereby Jesus gave up everything, even his life, for the sake of his brothers and sisters. When we see our celebration of the Eucharist as a commitment to follow Christ, who gave up everything for us, we do not see attending Mass as a central obligation of our faith but as a call to radical living. And it is that commitment that informs our spirituality, not the laws of the Church.

We could go through life not breaking any of the Church's laws and yet not living as Christians. Our Christianity demands more of us than adherence to the laws. It demands compassion of us. It demands that we reach out every day to our fellow-human beings and do what we can to alleviate their suffering.

Much of the suffering in the world that we are called to alleviate is caused by social and political structures that we may not even be fully aware of, but which we are called to identify as wrong and unjust and in need of dismantling. This is not easy. It was not easy to stand up against slavery in the past; it was not easy to oppose Nazism in the last century; it took a particular kind of insight and courage to stand against apartheid in South Africa.

Acts of defiance and rejection of unjust societal structures demand great courage from Christians, but they also demand a level of awareness about the nature of these unjust structures.

That is probably the hardest part. It can be very difficult for us to understand and get our heads around structural sin.

Part of the difficulty is our traditional understanding of sin, where it was clear who had sinned and who should repent. A sinful act carried out by a particular individual and the effect of that is clearly seen by others. But all the suffering caused by structures cannot be laid at the feet of any particular individual. It seems as though everybody and nobody is guilty. If there is nobody clearly to blame, then how can there be sin?

One of the frightening aspects of modern life is the extent to which we are all being held responsible for the injustices of our society without being conscious of it. We have accepted competitive success as normal in business, life, and even education. Those who reach the top succeed and those who don't are regarded as failures, inadequate and mainly seen as non-productive and treated accordingly.

In Ireland we are part of a society that allows over 10,000 people to stay homeless, and more than 1 in 3 are children. Nearly 140,000 children live in consistent poverty. I may not want it to happen, but I am part of a society which does not give children and adults a place to live and enough to live on, and we all share in the corporate responsibility.

The other problem is the complexity of the structures creates a kind of powerlessness in people, making them unsure what to do about them. What can I do about children working in sweatshop conditions that are thousands of miles away? What can I do to effect world trade organisations? What can I do to eliminate poverty and homelessness? If there is little I can do about it, how can I be sinful in not doing it? We can feel imprisoned, unable to escape from the structures or unable to do anything about them.

But there is even a bigger problem because the structural sin is legitimised and normalised and therefore it affects the way we see reality. Today, can you imagine that people would accept slavery? Yet they did, for hundreds and hundreds of years. The structures became so embedded in people's psyche that they did not see the sinfulness of the structure. Even St. Paul had no problem with slavery. That should make us suspect that we today are also living with structures that are unjust, but because they have become so much part of ourselves, we may not notice our sinfulness.

For example, I may regret that people are homeless but accept that it is inevitable and maybe even normal because of our economic system. Some people are poor because they just get left behind, some people are paid wages below the poverty line and I may believe that this is just the way capitalism works. I might even argue that capitalism requires a small pool of unemployed people. This is the way things work, this is the way things are, and there is nothing that I can do about it.

This is because the way our world is structured has become so embedded in our psyche that we may not even be able to perceive the wrongness of these structures. We may have internalised the injustice of the system. For example, a report form March 2018 on attitudes to diversity in Ireland has found that nearly half of Irish adults believe some cultures are superior to others, and about one in six believe that some races or ethnic groups were born less intelligent. This was reported in the press and nobody said boo. Every day we hear it being said that people on welfare have too good a time, they are too lazy to work, or that homeless people prefer freedom without responsibility. If those are the beliefs of such large numbers of people in this Christian country, then there is something wrong with the way we are practising our Christianity.

So we have internalised the unjust system and we accept these structures and really believe we are doing the right thing. That's what the Pharisees did when they handed Jesus over. They believed that they were doing the right thing. Such informed consciousness may regard the situation as inevitable, like homeless people and poor people are the will of God. The simple structure becomes part and parcel of ourselves, we become totally unaware of the sinfulness that inherently exists in the system and we can be convinced that we are upright Christians who live according to the Gospel.

If we are to live faithful to our Christian commitment, we need to totally reimagine that commitment, and we need to reinvent Irish society. When I think about the kind of Christian Catholic Ireland I would like to see, I envisage a place where any child could grow up safe and well and take their place as a responsible and participating citizen.

Let's imagine a child, then, born into a socially just Ireland. They might be born a boy or a girl, healthy or with HIV or a disability, born into an immigrant family or a Traveller family, in a town or a city, with a two-parent family or a single parent. Whatever the child's gender, health, genetic heritage, cultural identity or family, it is natural to want to give all babies love, security, safety, warmth, food and shelter. Nor is it hard to extend this thinking to all people and believe that everyone should be able to live free of violence, oppression and addiction, to be safe from trafficking, slavery and exploitation, and to have their health, housing, educational and economic needs met.

For that to happen, we require a needs-based housing, health and education provision as a right. That is the cornerstone of social justice and the least we should expect from a society that calls itself Christian.

On housing we have many pronouncements, but we have no visible strategy or policy to house the growing number of families and individuals who are being made homeless every day because of our total lack of provision for decent social and affordable housing. Instead we have relied and are relying on the market to provide accommodation. But the market is not interested in housing homeless people. The market has no concern for homelessness. The market has no conscience, and we cannot expect it to have a conscience.

We, however, as Church, pride ourselves on our conscience. Let us examine our conscience then and see where we are found wanting. Our conscience should be able to tell us that observing Church law is an insufficient commitment to Christian values. What we need is to turn our attention instead to developing our sense of Christian compassion.

If poverty itself is a serious barrier to social justice, the refusal by the well off to believe in the existence of poverty is an even more serious barrier, and it is up to the Church to identify this barrier to social justice and denounce it. The Church needs to challenge the thinking that says poor people are poor because they are lazy or stupid or drink too much. The myth that we have deserving and undeserving poor is the most insidious myth in our society. People are poor by and large because they are born poor. Though sometimes people are able to acquire funds and status through a combination of talent, hard work and good luck over time, poor people rarely become rich. One reason for this is that being poor is a full-time job in itself; but it is also because poverty, though it is defined largely in economic terms, has complex effects in every area of the life of the poor that make it almost impossible for them to move out of their poverty; effects like social exclusion, high educational drop-out rates and poor mental and physical health.

For this reason, it is up not to the individual but to society to eradicate poverty and give people of every income level the opportunity to participate fully in civic life. We need to change our thinking as a society and acknowledge that poverty cannot be measured in absolute terms; nor can a notional amount of money be identified as sufficient. What people need is not some arbitrary income; what they need is enough to live on. In other words, if we are to eradicate the grinding effects of poverty, we have to start by meeting people's actual needs.

Those are the social truths that should inform Church thinking. When the Church starts to think like this, the Church will start to act in a compassionate and socially radical way, but it first needs to reform its thinking and to change what it perceives to be its function in this society. Instead, we see a Church that is inward-looking, focused on its own problems and still, in spite of all the upheavals and trauma that the Church has experienced and caused, we have a Church that is marked more by its reiteration of Church law than by its commitment to compassion and more inclined to exclude people who do not conform to its ideas of law than accept them.

If we accept unjust structures we cease to be neutral, but when we accept our responsibility to change sinful structures that is a radical moment of grace. Pope Francis has proclaimed the Gospel in a way that is appropriate both to our world and to a culture that is radically changing. He is uncompromisingly supportive of the poor. He is calling to the Kingdom of God on Earth but his message is not filtering through to the people, and the Church is not being identified as a force for radical, compassionate change in the world.

When Jesus talked about the Kingdom he always talked in parables. He was not talking about something earth shattering; in fact when he describes it, the Kingdom is always something small. Think of, for example, the parable of the mustard seed, the tiniest of all seeds, the pearl of great price, the tiny pearl. It is like the treasure hidden in the field, and the Kingdom is not only always something small but it is also always hidden. So when we look for the coming of the Kingdom, we are not looking for some great big sign, we are looking for small things, small changes, small projects through which we are can try to improve the quality of life of those on the margins.

These projects reach out, trying to improve the lives of people who are poor or struggling through clearing up and speaking out against the unjust structures that are causing them. That is the true sign of the coming of the Kingdom of God.

Wherever we are living, wherever we are working, there we can help to build the Kingdom of God. Each one of us can get involved in those efforts to improve the quality of life of those around us and tackle the causes of injustice. And those efforts are the cornerstone on which the Kingdom is being built, creating a compassionate community.

Imagine thousands of these little lights of hope burning across the country, across each parish. A true sign of the Kingdom of Heaven on Earth.

I believe that my vision of a just, compassionate, caring Church is not an impossible dream. It is up to us all to think about it, talk about it and come up with the mechanisms for bringing about what amounts to a radical change. Knowing this is the work of the Holy Spirit and as we develop a new conscience for our time, we will find ways to speak out boldly like Jesus, and like Jesus, we will not care about the water we muddy along the way. A just, loving, caring and compassionate Church is not some sort of plateau that we can reach and from which point it will sustain itself. It is a constantly evolving process, and we can only bring it about by making a commitment to it and by continuing to plan for it in the future. This is not to deny the extraordinary work done by the Church in the area of compassion over the years and by priests and religious, but what I am writing about now is the official Church.

The time has come in our development to think long and hard about what it is that we want for our Church, how we are going to achieve what we want, and how we are going to put in place the mechanisms for change.

We are all the Church, we are all the people of God and we possess huge power, the power and dynamism of the Gospel and the Holy Spirit, and it is up to us to make it relevant today.

The Roman Catholic Church as we know it today will die out, but a new Church with the laity exercising their rightful place will emerge. But we must start now to enable it to happen.

It may not become a bigger Church, but we will become a stronger one with enormous joy, prayer, love, compassion, influence and impact.

'NEARER MY GOD TO THEE'–AND THE BAND PLAYED ON

FR MARK PATRICK HEDERMAN

My mother, Josephine Mullaney (1907-1987), was born in Boston, Massachusetts. For whatever reason, she went to Trinity College, Dublin to study for an arts degree. She was invited to spend some days at a farm in Co. Limerick, where my father, who was the youngest boy in that family, fell in love with her as she was getting out of the car. He knew she was only staying the weekend and he might never see her again, so he plucked up his courage and asked her to marry him. "I know nothing about you," she said, somewhat dismissively. "Well," came the jaunty reply. "You know as much about me now as you're ever going to know, so, you'd better make up your mind."

So, that's how I came to be born on a farm in Co. Limerick, Ireland in 1944. Now, I didn't realise at the time how great a privilege it was for me to be born into the most perfect body politic that had ever been devised on this planet since the Garden of Eden. Our little country, which had only recently shaken off the shackles of colonial serfdom, had become the most perfect manifestation of a Catholic country since the Acts of the Apostles.

There can be no doubt about it: there are moments in history when destiny calls and certain countries get the opportunity to reinvent themselves. A few examples are America with the Declaration of Independence in 1776, France after their Revolution in 1798, Russia after 1917, and here in Ireland during the first half of the 20th century. This was our opportunity to define what we meant by human being and put that into practice in a perfectly restructured socio-political entity, which we could call our own. The declaration of a republic in 1949 completed the process, which had begun much earlier of course, but had never been able to reach such perfection.

A year later as the 1950s began, the pudding, you might say, had set. Ireland was 'the most Catholic country in the world', according to Dr James Devane, who wrote in *The Irish Rosary* in 1952, "[p]erhaps the Republic of Ireland, as it is constituted today, is the only integral Catholic state in the world; a Catholic culture as it existed in the Middle Ages."[2] 93% of the population were practicing Roman Catholics: this meant weekly [often daily] attendance at Mass, pilgrimages, novenas, the rosary, Marian devotions, the Nine First Fridays, and of course the St Martin de Porres 'Black Babies' box in every pub and every shop, with the Catholic Truth Society stall at the back of every church, to give orthodox guidance to the faithful on all the thorny issues of the day.[3]

In 1948, when I was four, the then-Taoiseach of the coun-

2 Louise Fuller (2005). 'Religion, politics and socio-cultural change in twentieth century Ireland', *The European Legacy*, 10:1, 41-54, DOI: 10.1080/1084877052000321976.

3 Ibid.

try, John A. Costello sent a message to Pope Pius XII assuring him in the name of his cabinet colleagues of their 'filial loyalty' and their 'firm resolve to be guided in all [their] work by the teaching of Christ and to strive for the attainment of a social order based on Christian principles'. Many Irish politicians saw themselves as Catholics first and legislators second.

The impression of Ireland held in Rome in the early 1950s was of a country that had preserved a purity of faith in the face of persecution and famine, a country loyal to Rome, in which the combined might of the apparatus of Church and State was exercised in keeping at bay the kind of modern influences which were perceived as undermining the Christian heritage.[4]

On the 10th of April 1951, a letter was received by the Secretary of the Congress of Irish Unions from Monsignor Montini, Substitute Papal Secretary of State and future Pope Paul VI, acknowledging the address of homage and the chasuble presented to Pope Pius XII during the Holy Year in the name of the workers of Ireland. The letter, as recorded in the Irish Catholic Directory in 1952, read as follows:

"At a time when so many of the workers of various countries have fallen prey to false theories and ideologies that are in direct contrast to the Christian religion, it was a source of particular gratification to His Holiness to receive this further proof of the devoted attachment of the workers of Ireland to the Vicar of Christ, and to their fidelity to the Catholic Faith, which is their nation's most precious heritage."

4   Louise Fuller (2005). 'Religion, politics and socio-cultural change in twentieth century Ireland', *The European Legacy*, 10:1, 41-54, DOI: 10.1080/1084877052000321976.

If Rome were to issue rosettes for winners of the prize for being the most Catholic country in Europe during the first half of the 20th Century, then Ireland would definitely have won the red rosette for first place. Franco's Spain might have come second, and Salazar's Portugal a close third.

Of course no one would ever dream of suggesting that the Irish Free State was a theocracy, but with a certain amount of 'mental reservation', to borrow a phrase, one could say that in the 1950s this country was Catholicism 'effectively transformed into a civil theology'.[5] "And so, during the first fifty years of independence, leaders of both Church and State, irrespective of political party, shared a desire to develop the country according to a philosophy of Catholic nationalism."[6]

In 1937 the so-called De Valera Constitution of our 'free' state, expressed this derived philosophy in legal terms. In a radio broadcast to the United States on the 15th of June that same year, De Valera called it "the spiritual and cultural embodiment of the Irish people" and to mark its first anniversary in 1938, he reminded us that: "As faith without good works is dead, so must we expect our Constitution to be if we are content to leave it merely as an idle statement of principles in which we profess belief but have not the will to put into practice." Sean O'Faolain described De Valera's philosophy as "something so dismal that beside it the Trappist Rule of Mount Melleray is a Babylonian orgy".

Although it is true that all over Europe after The Great War

....

5   D.V. Twomey, *The End of Irish Catholicism*? Dublin, Veritas, 2003, p. 33 (quoted in Daithí Ó Corráin, Op.cit., p 733.)

6   Daithí Ó Corráin, Op. cit., p 733.

there was a fear of degenerate moral behaviour, Ireland in its new Republic was particularly single-minded and fanatical about establishing a national dugout. The Church and the government in Ireland became obsessed with warding off the threat to Catholic purity from foreign, especially English and American, influences. There was a naïve popular belief that if left alone, Ireland would be a paradise. Our little island of purity was surrounded by a sea of vice. It was everyone's job to keep the slurry from our shores. As J. Keirn Brennan and Ernest R. Ball said in their poem 'A Little Bit of Heaven', "Sure a little bit of heaven fell from out the sky one day, and it nestled in the ocean in a place so far away and when the angels found it sure it looked so sweet and fair they said suppose we leave it for it looks so peaceful there."

Now I, of course, did not realise the great privilege of mine to be born into this dugout instead of in some god-forsaken metropolis of 'pagan' America, for instance. American movies became enemy number one. As James Montgomery, the appointed censor of films from 1923 to 1940, often said: "one of the greatest dangers of . . . films is not the Anglicisation of Ireland, but its Los Angelesisation." The 1923 Censorship of Films act was aimed directly at the 'Harlotry of Hollywood'. Films banned in Ireland included The Marx Brothers in *Monkey Business*, Charlie Chaplin's *The Great Dictator* [Ireland being neutral at the time did not want to offend Adolf Hitler] and Joseph Strick's attempt to put Joyce's *Ulysses* on the screen. As one playwright put it: "I wrote a three-act comedy but when the censors were finished it had become a one-act tragedy."

Such ideologies won their major victory in the Censorship of Publications Act of 1929. By 1943, the year before I was born, over 2,000 books had been banned including those by Saul Bellow, William Faulkner, H.G. Wells and Emile Zola. Irish authors from Liam O'Flaherty in the 1930s to Lee Dunne in the 1970s began to worry that they weren't banned -- it seemed to cast aspersions on their artistry. On the proscribed list were: Frank O'Connor, Austin Clarke, the two Nobel prize winners Beckett and Shaw, and, of course, both Edna and Kate O'Brien.

The full impact of my entitlement as a citizen of this bastion of beatitude did not become apparent to me until sometime later when I reached the age of reason, as they say. In the early 1950s, I was handed my guide book to correct living in this perfect paradise: *A Catechism of Catholic Doctrine*, published by Gill & Son in 1951, approved by the archbishops and bishops of Ireland and with an imprimatur from John Charles McQuaid. It answered every single question you might think of from 'Who made the world?' to 'How should we prepare for extreme unction?' There was no need to worry our heads about existentialism and the other diseases that afflicted the rest of the world; we had our *Vade Mecum*, which was for teaching in all primary schools where children were required to memorise each prescribed answer by rote. I began to share John McGahern's concern: "When I was in my 20s it did occur to me that there was something perverted about an attitude that thought that killing somebody was a minor offence compared to kissing somebody." How did all this come about? How was it possible?

We were an island. We were impervious. To make the point, let me tell you another story. In 1936, my mother came over to Ireland on the Cunard Line from America. Everybody in America knew that Edward VIII, King of England, was having an affair with Mrs Wallace Simpson. It was all over the newspapers, with photographs of the pair. In Ireland, and indeed England, when my mother arrived, nobody knew about it. It was a secret. The government had forbidden the press to publish this news; it was considered dangerous to national security, and the press obeyed. When my mother began to tell people at parties in Dublin, they thought she was off her head. Being a conscientious Catholic, she asked a Jesuit priest whether it was libel to be spreading news that was common knowledge in America but completely unknown over here. "I'm not quite sure which it is," he said, "but it's very interesting. Tell me more."

And if stories are not enough, let me quote from the recently published *Cambridge History of Ireland* in four volumes: "The power of religion peaked in the 1950s by which time the Catholic Church had become a lazy monopoly, the legacy of which is proving to be its greatest burden. The decline in the authority and pre-eminent position of the Catholic Church, the rise of secularism and the beginnings of the effort to dismantle legislative and constitutional support for a Catholic ethos can be traced to the early 1960s."[7] 'The Swinging Sixties', as they are sometimes called, destroyed the dream. That 'hideous decade', in the words of its detractors, introduced the virus that proved lethal. I haven't time in this short essay to give you the details, but let me summarise in an acronym of three letters: HIV stands, in this case, for: the Hippie movement, Information Technology and Vatican II.

'Make Love Not War', one of the catch-cries of the hippies, emerged from the United States in the early 1960s and

....

7   Daithí Ó Corráin, Ibid, p 727.

spawned worldwide. Young people were no longer prepared to obey their elders and be coerced into joining armies and fighting wars that had destroyed previous generations. Protests against the US military involvement in Vietnam, the Woodstock Music and Art Festival in New York, the Summer of Love in San Francisco, were milestones of the movement. Irish bishops had foreseen this and had prophesied: "Company keeping under the stars of night has succeeded in too many places to the good old Irish custom of visiting, chatting and story-telling from one house to another, with the rosary to bring all home in due time." A joint pastoral of 1927 had warned: "The evil one is forever setting his snares for unwary feet. At the moment, his traps for the innocent are chiefly the dance-hall, the bad book, the indecent paper, the motion picture, the immodest fashion in female dress - all of which tend to destroy the characteristic virtues of our race." The eye of the storm was information technology, and nothing can compare with the ravages of RTÉ. Oliver James Flanagan, TD for Laois-Offaly from 1943 to 1987, claimed famously that "there was no sex in Ireland before television". Whereas Radio Éireann, first transmitted in 1926, did all in its power to reinforce the Catholic ethos of the country, Telefís Eireann, from its beginnings on New Year's Eve 1961, did everything in its power to undermine Catholic Ireland.

Gay Byrne, a name synonymous with Irish radio and television, joined Radio Éireann in 1958 and was on our TV screens for the rest of the century. He was the first host of *The Late Late Show*, the world's longest-running chat show, presenting it from 1962 to 1999. Until then, matters of personal intimacy were unheard of as topics of public discourse in this country.

One evening Gay Byrne picked a married couple from the audience, and asked each of them a series of questions while the other was out of earshot. One of the questions related to the colour of Eileen's nightie on their honeymoon. The husband said it was transparent, the wife said she wasn't wearing one. Thomas Ryan, Bishop of Clonfert in Galway, issued an immediate statement to the *Sunday Press*, who gave it front-page treatment the following morning. In his sermon at eight o'clock Mass the following morning at St Brendan's Cathedral in Loughrea, the bishop urged his congregation to register its protest "in any manner you think fit, so as to show the producers in Irish television, that you, as decent Catholics, will not tolerate programmes of this nature". There were angry letters to the papers for weeks afterwards. One letter invited readers to West Cork, where it was claimed that all wore corduroys in bed.

As for the third deadly blow of the 1960s – the 'v' in the virus, it came within the very bosom of the Church itself: Vatican II. One eminent personage described the three greatest disasters of the 20th Century as: Hitler, DeValera, and Pope John XXIII.

The Vatican Council that sought to reform Catholicism was almost completely lost on the leadership of Irish Catholicism. In a famous sermon at the Pro-Cathedral in Dublin, John Charles McQuaid, returning from Rome after the council, said: "You may have been worried by much talk of changes to come. Allow me to reassure you. No change will worry the tranquillity of your Christian lives."[8]

8   John Cooney. *John Charles McQuaid: Ruler of Catholic Ireland*, O'Brien Press, 1999, p 371.

What we experienced in the second half of the 20th century was a double earthquake: the Vatican Council and the Sexual Revolution. As John McGahern again suggests: "Ireland is a peculiar society in the sense that it was a 19th century society up to about 1970 and then it almost bypassed the twentieth century." By the time Pope John Paul II made his famous visit to Ireland in 1979, far from being a triumphant display of 2.7 million Catholics turning out to greet him, it was a last ditch stand for Roman Catholic Ireland. In 1979, after two decades of rapid economic growth, openness to the outside world, and sweeping universal cultural change, the Catholic Church in Ireland was in serious trouble. The openly acknowledged purpose of the Irish hierarchy in inviting John Paul II to Ireland was to halt or at least slow down the damaging inroads to the ancient Catholic faith of Ireland.[9]

Let me make three things clear before I go on to tell you what I really think about our present situation. Number one is this: Jesus Christ has already saved the whole world without much help from us, and often in spite of the Church he founded to carry on the good work. Number two: God does not step away from the forms and structures that God has instituted; unless, and this is the great mystery of free will, unless we ourselves remove them from God. And number three: The Holy Spirit of God is with the Church of Jesus Christ until the end of time. The real question is: are we?

This book's full title could read: 'Five Years to save the Irish Roman Catholic Church.' The title of my essay is "Nearer my

---

9   Thomas Bartlett, *The Cambridge History of Ireland, 1880 to the Present*, Volume IV, Cambridge University Press, 2018, p xxxi.

God to Thee' and the band played on'. There are two reasons for this title: this was the hymn they were singing and the band was playing as the Titanic sank; and, in itself, it is a very beautiful hymn, which, if you listen to the words, tells you all you need to know: 'nearer my God to thee'.

How do we here in Ireland in this 21st century get nearer to our God? That is the only really important question. At the moment, in our Church, we are three steps away from that goal. The Irish Roman Catholic Church is at present three carriages away from the engine. How do we uncouple ourselves from the two carriages that are getting in the way: the Roman and the Irish?

The first carriage, or rather the last, has already been dislodged and is hurtling its way down some cliff, like the herd of swine after the exorcism of the Gaderene demoniac in the Gospel of St Luke Chapter Eight. And who is not glad to see the back of the claustrophobic Irish Catholic Church of the 1950s? I certainly am not. Good riddance, I say. I cannot believe that the monolithic Ireland of that period has crumbled into dust. I don't really care what the causes were of the disappearance of the melting iceberg that was 1950s Irish Catholicism – I just look around me in delight and in disbelief, revelling in the exhilaration that it is now gone. Now the job is to try to uncouple ourselves from the middle carriage which comes between us and the Church that Christ intended to found. This is the 'Roman' part of that Irish Roman Catholic trio. The Church at present is not simply an 'Empire of Misogyny', to borrow a phrase; rather, it is, more accurately and critically, a protectorate of priesthood, a pyramid, as the Pharaohs built them on the backs of slaves in Egypt, of Pharisaic hierarchy. Hierarchy is a paradigm that remains endemic to anything Roman, and it will require much resilience and ingenuity to remove it as a brand mark from those who follow Jesus Christ in the Catholic Church. Canon 1299 of the fairly recently *Revised Code of Canon Law* (1983), specifies that only those who have received sacred orders are qualified for governance in the Church, also called the power of jurisdiction.[10] The canon further stipulates that although lay members of the Christian faithful can cooperate in the exercise of this same power, they cannot wield it in any significant way because, legally speaking, 'cooperate' does not mean 'participate'. Such is the view of Ladislas Orsy, expert in canon law, who himself attended the Second Vatican Council.

This is a matter separate and different from the question of women's ordination. What we are talking about is the complete 'clericalisation' of the Church. Whether priests are men or women, or both, we cannot have a situation where only priests can exercise power. This amounts to a clerical oligarchy where lay people have no say in matters of legislation or governance and no real or effective participation in the running of the Church. Pope Francis seems to be trying to effect such an uncoupling as best he can, but it is difficult, and Bergoglio is not Steve McQueen. Stretching the image, we might say that the old link and pin design which used to work in the days of

10 Can. 129 §1. Those who have received sacred orders are qualified according to the norms of the prescripts of the law, for the power of governance, which exists in the Church by divine institution and is also called the power of jurisdiction.§2. Lay members of the Christian faithful can cooperate in the exercise of this same power according to the norm of law.

the Great Train Robbery has been replaced by a much more effective and resistant AAR-type knuckle coupler patented in the Vatican. The carriages are joined to the engine almost inflexibly. The Vatican and the Church have become identified. But let us remember that the Vatican itself as we know it today is a very recent invention. Although the name comes from and is almost as ancient as the hills surrounding Rome, the bureaucratic entity that is the organisational hub of the 1.2 billion Catholics around the world came into being less than a hundred years ago.

When King Victor Emmanuel II took back power from the Pope in 1870, and Rome became what it is today (Italy's capital city), some compensation had to be made to the Catholic Church, which had already lost all its territories to the Kingdom of Italy by 1860. The Lateran Treaty of 1929, which brought the Vatican city-state into existence, provided such an opportunity. The treaty spoke of the Vatican as a new creation, and not as the remnant of the former Papal States, which extended throughout most of central Italy from 756 to 1870. Vatican City was a compromise and a milksop to allow the Holy See the political benefits of territorial sovereignty. The treaty was signed by the Cardinal Secretary of State, Pietro Gasparri, on behalf of the Holy See, and by Prime Minister Benito Mussolini on behalf of the Kingdom of Italy on June 7th 1929. The golden pen used for the signing, later presented to Il Duce, was supplied by Pope Pius himself. And so the Vatican as we know it today was born: a landlocked sovereign city-state within the city of Rome itself. It has approximately 110 acres and a population of about 800 people. It includes St. Peter's

Square, which is marked off from the territory of Italy by a simple white line. White lines should be possible to erase.

Pope Francis, as I understand things, is trying to effect a velvet revolution in the world-wide Church. He is trying to turn an oligarchical model into what he calls a 'synodal' one, where all members would be consulted and have their voices heard; where every topic can be aired and free discussion can be encouraged. Can this Pope effect such changes? There are powerful forces working against this slim possibility. Many inside and outside the Catholic Church are hoping that Pope Francis won't last very long. His health is not great so he might die of natural causes; if not, there are other ways of getting rid of him as Pope. One of these would be trial for heresy. If Pope Francis is contradicting the words and the teachings of Our Lord Jesus Christ, then he has no place on the throne of Peter. At least four cardinals have submitted a series of questions - known as '*dubia*' - to the Pope over his apostolic exhortation, *Amoris Laetitia*. A separate group of theologians, academics and priests have issued what they call 'a filial correction,' in Latin, the official language of the Church, to the Pope, accusing him of supporting views on 'marriage, the moral life and the Eucharist' which break with Catholic teaching. Others bring more virulent accusations of heresy or apostasy which, if proven, would require the abdication of the Pope. A sample few: "Antipope Francis says that Judas may not be in Hell; Antipope Francis says that Muslims are genuine believers; Antipope Francis says he celebrated Martin Luther's Reformation; Antipope Francis believes that you can live in adultery, be in a state of grace, and receive holy communion." Can one man pit himself against the deeply entrenched conservatism of one of the largest and oldest religious institutions in the world? Marco Politi, an experienced Vatican commentator, gives an account of the opposition, including many, though not all, of the curia. In his book, *Francis among the Wolves: The Inside Story of a Revolution*, he claims that there is opposition in Italy and in the USA where "there exists a robust network of Catholic universities, colleges, and lobbies that, in parallel to conservative American Protestantism, consider a traditionalist outlook on faith essential to the moral health of the United States".[11] Joshua Lisa Sowle Cahill, an eminent moral theologian, describes Francis as using "the synod process as a way to consider possible developments in Church teaching without causing open divisions in the Church".

St Augustine, writing in the 4th and 5th century, identifies two churches in one: the inner Church of St John (the 'heart' of the Church), which is distinct from the outer Church of St Peter (the 'head' of the Church)[12]:

The Church knows two lives which have been laid down and commended to her by God. One is through faith, the other through vision. The apostle Peter personifies the first life, John the second. The first has no place except on Earth; it lasts only to the end of the present age and comes to an end in the next world. The second life has no end in the age to come, and its perfection is delayed until the end of the present age. . . sub-

11   Marco Politi. *Francis Among the Wolves: The Inside Story of a Revolution*, Columbia University Press, 2015, p. 165.

12   St Augustine on St John's Gospel, Homily 124: 5,7.

lime knowledge proclaimed by John concerning the Trinity and unity of the whole godhead, which in His kingdom we shall see face to face, but now, until the Lord comes, we must behold in a glass darkly. It was not only John who drank: the Lord himself has spread John's gospel throughout the world, so that according to each one's capacity all people may drink it.

We are all beneficiaries of this second Church, this inner Church, this mystical connection with God. Nothing and nobody can separate us from the love of God. The Catholic Church is not simply an organisation; it is more properly described as an organism. That is: it is not simply constituted by the world-wide multi-national organisation it has become; it is alive and well and fully present in each part of itself wherever "two or three are gathered in my name."[13] Every local church in Ireland is a Temple of the Lord. Every person in this country is potentially a dwelling-place of the Holy Spirit.

What might a 'Catholic' Church look like that was really 'Catholic' – meaning fully open, all-inclusive, universal? And what would it look like shorn of its first class carriage reserved for the Irish team, or any other localised national ghetto? My hope would be that such a slimmed down programme might make our Church look a bit more like it 'was in the beginning, is now, and ever shall be, world without end, amen'.

---

13   Matthew, 18:20.

THE CATHOLIC CHURCH'S HOME GROWN EXISTENTIAL CRISIS

MARY MCALEESE

Today and every single day this year at least thirty-seven thousand new Catholics will be created by Baptism. They will join the biggest Christian denomination in the world, with a Church membership of almost 1.3 billion people. One in six of the planet's entire population is a member of the Catholic Church. Members are spread unevenly across five continents: 48% in the Americas, 23% in Europe, 17% in Africa, 11% in Asia and 1% in Oceania. Half of all the world's Christians are Catholics.[14] The Catholic Church is the biggest global non-governmental provider of education, healthcare, charitable and welfare services, especially to the poor, which is among the reasons why of all the world's faith systems, only it enjoys Permanent Observer status at the United Nations. It educates 66 million children in 200,000 schools worldwide and the majority of

----

14 *Annuarium Statisticum Ecclesiae*, Vatican Publishing House, 2015.

these children are not themselves Catholic. [15]

The number of Catholics worldwide is growing at a rate much faster than the rate of growth of the world population.[16] The greatest increase is occurring in Africa, where the number of Catholics grew by over 41% in the past decade. One hundred years ago there were 291 million Catholics in the world. There are five times as many today, well ahead of the world population growth over the same period.

So is it really possible that an institution experiencing such exponential growth and with a formidable universal presence could simultaneously be in potentially terminal decline in its very heartland of Ireland, in a country which has been Christianised for fifteen centuries; a country whose medieval missionary monks saved Christianity and European civilization itself from obliteration in the Dark Ages that followed the fall of the Roman Empire[17]; a country which today boasts 78% of the population as members of the Catholic Church?

....

15 Committee on the Rights of the Child (CRC), Summary record of the 1852nd meeting of 16 Jan 2014. Discussion of the Holy See's Second Periodic Report on the United Nations Convention on the Rights of the Child (UNCRC), 27. Archbishop Silvano Maria Tomasi, then Permanent Observer of the Holy See Mission to the UN (Geneva), is reported in a non-verbatim summary to have told the CRC that 60% of pupils in Catholic Schools did not profess the Catholic faith. All records of the Holy See's engagement with the CRC are available from the website of the United Nations Human Rights Office of the High Commissioner at http://tbinternet.ohchr.org/_layouts/TreatyBodyExternal/Countries.aspx? CountryCode=VAT&Lang=EN

16 *Annuarium Statisticum Ecclesiae*, Vatican Publishing House, 2014.

17 Thomas Cahill, *How the Irish Saved Civilisation*, Nan A. Talese, 1995.

From where could come an existential threat to such a formidable and enduring presence not just in Ireland, but also in the world? How realistic is the doomsday scenario in this book's theme of five years to save the Irish Church? The answer is that yes, there is a serious existential threat. The bad news is that it is most evident in the very places where the Church has been present and strongest for the longest time. The younger Church in Africa and Asia is characterised by growth in numbers, including the number of priests. The older Church here and in the West in general is characterised by a decline in practice and vocations that has not been halted by the so-called 'Francis factor'.[18] The good news is that the threat comes mainly from within, and thus it is within the abilities of the Church to address and redress it if it has a mind to. Appropriate action by the Church could yet transform the current decline, from an existential threat into a healthy transition to a Church worthy of its founder. However, with external pressures and internal disenchantment far outpacing internal reform, there are as yet no convincing signs the Church's leaders have a clear grasp of where the problems and their solutions lie.

I want to argue that the biggest existential threat to the Church comes from fundamental design flaws in its own structure, which are largely overlooked thanks to a culture that is practiced at critiquing the external world but slow to turn the

18   Pew Forum, 'Pope Francis Still Highly Regarded in U.S., but Signs of Disenchantment Emerge', 2 March 2018 (quoting results from January 2015 survey conducted by Pew Research Center), http://www.pewforum.org/2018/03/06/pope-francis-still-highly-regarded-in-u-s-but-signs-of-disenchantment-emerge/

spotlight internally. The Church is suffering from the ecclesiastical equivalent of mental fatigue. It may look strong, it may even be flying brand new 'planes' in some places, but a close examination, particularly of the older churches in the fleet, reveals an accumulation of repeated stresses which have not been properly addressed or rectified and which have produced a myriad of cracks. Their overall structure has been gradually weakened. In the Western World, the historical engine of Christianity, there is a growing risk of the engine stalling in a number of countries, Ireland among them. Engine failure could come from a stress which on its own would not normally be strong enough to produce a catastrophic fracture, but which on a weakened structure may be all that is required to create total destruction. The domino effect could course rapidly through the Universal Church precisely because it is universal.

We could argue all day about how much time the Church has to successfully address the problem – five, fifty, five hundred years. Since the Church is experienced differently and has vastly different contexts across the five continents in which it operates, what is valid for Ireland may not be valid for other countries or cultures. We could shrug and point to the strong belief that Christ has promised to be with the Church till the end of time, no matter how big a mess is made of it. But that would ignore our role as the hands of His work in making the Church fit and proper for the purpose Christ intended. We could also argue about what it would take to successfully address the existential problem it faces, reciting a list of contemporary contentious issues such as the Church's role in fueling sexism and homophobia, its teachings on artificial contraception, the lack of access to the sacraments for the divorced and remarried, inter-communion, the silencing of conscientious and especially scholarly dissent, the failure to draw obvious lessons from dwindling recruitment to the priesthood in the West, the failure to truly engage and empower the laity at every level of the Church, the erratic responses to the child protection and episcopal management issues revealed by the scandals of Catholic institutional and clerical child abuse, and the list goes on.

In one way the debates on these issues, no matter how fractious or unresolved, are evidence of a dynamic anxiety among some of the *Christifideles* to ensure the authenticity of the Catholic faith in today's world. They are evidence of a determination that the Church will not be paralysed by appeals to a hermeneutic of continuity which, in response to so many issues, paints a picture of an unchanging two thousand year orthodoxy which never existed in reality and which, if it had, would have ensured the Church's demise long ago. Some prefer to ignore the historical truth that the Church has often backed itself into untenable doctrinal positions, taught them for decades, even centuries, only to quietly reverse out of them, usually without apology. Galileo is only the tip of a very large iceberg. We do not have to go too far back to trip over some of the more egregious examples. In 1930 Pope Pius XI described the advocates of the emancipation and equality of women as "false teachers".[19]

But I want to go back to the year 1858, the year of the famous

19 Pope Pius XI, *Casti connubii*, 31 Dec. 1930, note 74, in AAS 22 (1930) 539-598).

apparitions at Lourdes which we all heard about at school, to an event which we did not hear about: the abduction of a six-year-old Jewish boy Edgardo Mortara on the authority of Pope Pius IX. It is an event that makes the point about how an inherently flawed, but outwardly strong structure can be fatally undermined by the straw that broke the camel's back. Edgardo was that straw. Pius IX, the longest serving Pope in the history of the papacy, was also the secular sovereign ruler of the Papal States. He was the Pope who in 1870 presided over the First Vatican Council, which declared the doctrine of papal infallibility. In 1870 he also presided over the complete disintegration of the Papal States and the end of the Pope's temporal power, which had lasted for a thousand years. The abduction and forced baptisms of non-Christian children were not unusual in the Papal States, but historians now recognise that it was likely the abduction of six-year-old Edgardo Mortara that helped, along with other political factors, to precipitate the final demise of the Pope's temporal power.[20]

Edgardo was one of a Jewish family of eight children living in Bologna. He was taken violently from his home by forces from Church Inquisition and brought to Rome in June 1858. This was allegedly because he had been secretly baptised by the family's Catholic housemaid. Church teaching at that time insisted a Catholic child could not be raised by non-Catholics, even if they were his or her parents. Pope Pius IX refused to return the child to his distraught parents and effectively made himself the child's guardian. Edgardo was neither the first nor

20 Marina Caffiero. *Forced Baptisms: History of Jews, Christians and Converts in Papal Rome*, trans. by Lydia Cochrane, University of California Press, 2012.

last Jewish child to be treated this way by the Church, but what differentiates his story from all others is the sheer effort expended by his traumatised parents in order to get him back, and the huge international outcry that made his abduction a cause célèbre.

Edgardo never did return home, and the intransigence of Pius IX in keeping the child from his parents is now credited with weakening support among the allies he depended on to protect the Papal States, to the extent that they were overrun and overwhelmed. It was sixty years before the Church finally accepted that there would be no return to the model of Church as both a spiritual and secular empire. It is a telling story long since conveniently overlooked by the Church and only today being revisited by scholars and accorded its proper place in the narrative not just of Church history, but the history of the establishment of a secular state in Italy.[21]

The fundamental design flaw in the Church of the 19th century that Edgardo's story highlighted was the insistence in Church teaching that God had created the Church to be both the world's sole spiritual and temporal source of governance.[22] Such was declared to be its right and its destiny by Gregory XVI in 1832, and in the same encyclical he also asked whether anyone sane could possibly believe in the idea of freedom of

....

21 David Kertzer. *The Kidnapping of Edgardo Mortara*, Picador, 1997.

22 Joseph G. Trabbic, 'Did Vatican II endorse separation of Church and State?' *Crisis*, 9 January 2015, https://www.crisismagazine.com/2015/vatican-ii-separation-church-state-rupture-continuity.

conscience.[23] The Church alone claimed the right to inform the consciences of the public.

Today another fundamental design flaw is quietly but perceptibly eroding the Church's basic infrastructure. That flaw rests on a clash between Church law and international human rights law, as the latter has developed since the second half of the 20th century. International human rights law has changed the context in which many Catholics live and experience their faith. It is inexorably changing the way Catholics, particularly in advanced democracies, look at their allegiance to the Church and their obedience to its teachings.

Nobody is born a Catholic. One usually becomes a Catholic by baptism in the Catholic Church.[24] Baptism has numerous and complex effects. Some are spiritual/theological[25] like being freed from original sin; others are legal/canonical like enrolment as a lifelong member of the Catholic Church[26] with all

....

23 Pope Gregory XVI, *Mirari Vos*, 15 August 1832, note 5, in ASS 4 (1868) 336-345.

24 It is possible to become a member of the Catholic Church by 'reception' into the Church having been previously baptised in a Christian denomination which is not in communion with the Catholic Church but whose baptisms are recognised as valid by the Catholic Church.

25 Code of Canon Law 1983, canon 849 explains that by Baptism a child is freed from all sins including original sin, born again as a child of God, made like to Christ by an indelible character and incorporated into the Church.

26 Code of Canon Law 1983, canon 96 provides that by Baptism a person is incorporated into the Church of Christ and is constituted *a persona* (person) in it, which means acquiring a juridic personhood in canon law with consequent juridical/canonical rights and obligations (also cf. canons 11;111 §1; §2).

the rights and obligations of membership. The Church teaches *semel Catholicus semper Catholicus* (once a Catholic always a Catholic). It teaches that from the age of seven, with the use of reason, one is bound by Church law.[27] It teaches that members are obliged to be obedient to Church teachings in ways that affect the roles they play and positions they advocate in the secular world, including in the workplace and in public and political life.[28]

International human rights law since the Universal Declaration of Human Rights or UHDR (1949), on the other hand, says that every human being has the right to freedom of thought, conscience, belief, and religion, including the right to change religion.[29] Today many people who were baptised into the Catholic Church are simply exercising their human right to walk away, to change religion or to give up on religion altogether. They no longer believe in the legitimacy of the principle *semel Catholicus semper Catholicus*, a principle that seems

....

27   Cf. Code of Canon Law 1983, canon 11.

28   Congregation for the Doctrine of Faith, instruction *Donum veritatis,* note 39 24 May 1990, *AAS* 82 (1990) 1557.

29   Cf. Universal Declaration of Human Rights 1949, Article 18. "Everyone has the right to freedom of thought, conscience and religion; this right includes freedom to change his religion or belief". The European Convention on Human Rights (ECHR) makes exactly the same statement and binds members of the Council of Europe, of which the Holy See is not a member. Since the Treaty of Lisbon 2009, the E.U. Charter of Fundamental Rights binds E.U. institutions and member states. Art. 10.1 says, "Everyone has the right to freedom of thought, conscience and religion. This right includes freedom to change religion or belief." The Holy See is not a member of the European Union nor is the Vatican City State.

incompatible with the fundamental freedoms set out in the UDHR and other human rights guidelines.

Other people remain within the Church even while conscientiously disagreeing with some Church teachings. The human rights of Church members to freedom of conscience, opinion and belief are not reflected in Church law. Instead, those rights are heavily restricted by the obligations of obedience to the magisterium[30] and the importance of maintaining communion with the Church.[31] And this is where the Church's flawed structure is most at risk, as the vast majority of Catholics had those obligations and those restrictions on their fundamental freedoms imposed on them when they were baptised as infants and from the moment of their baptism, their consent is presumed, and for the rest of their lives, even when they are able to give informed consent, they will never be asked to formally validate or repudiate their Church membership, but will instead be treated as if they had voluntarily given personal fully informed consent at Baptism.

Infant baptism is normative in the Church-- in fact it is demanded of Catholic parents. They are obliged to see to it that their infants are baptised within the first few weeks of birth.[32] In 1980 the Congregation of the Doctrine of the Faith (CDF) rejected the idea of postponing Baptism until a child could make an informed choice.[33] It defended the practice of

30 Code of Canon Law 1983, canon 212 §1.

31 Code of Canon Law 1983, canon 209 §1.

32 Code of Canon Law 1983, canon 867 §1.

33 Congregation for the Doctrine of the Faith, instruction on infant baptism Pastoralis actio, note 13, 20 October 1980, AAS 72 (1980) 1137-1156.

infant baptism, saying it conferred important spiritual bene-fits on the child and did not restrict its freedom.[34] What the Congregation failed to consider, however, was whether a baby could be baptised and benefit from the so-called indel-ible spiritual consequences of Baptism, which accrue *ex opere operato Christi*, without necessarily being enrolled for life as a Church member. Could they not become part of the body of Christ and have original sin expunged at Baptism without becoming enrolled as permanent members of the Catholic Church? Could permanent membership be postponed until a time when they could understand its implications? The sepa-ration of the spiritual effects of Baptism from the juridical con-sequences of being enrolled as a Church member did not occur to the CDF. Yet consideration of this separation is essential if the human rights of the child and the rights of adults baptised as infants are to be honoured within the Church.

In 2007, the Catholic Church's International Theological Commission wrote of infant baptism that there is a "lack of free-will and responsible choice on the part of infants".[35] The choice of Baptism and its automatic Church membership is made for children by their parents and the Church. International chil-dren's rights law acknowledges the right of parents "to provide direction to the child in the exercise of his or her right to free-dom of conscience, opinion and religion in a manner consistent

----

34 Congregation for the Doctrine of the Faith, instruction *Pastoralis actio*, notes 2; 21, 20 October 1980, *AAS* 72 (1980) 1137-1156.

35 International Theological Commission, 'The Hope of Salvation for Infants Who Die Without Being Baptised', 2007, 93.

with the evolving capacities of the child".[36] This right of parents to provide direction to a child has to be seen over and against the child's right to freedom of conscience, opinion and religion. Precisely when the child's mental capacities are sufficiently evolved to shift agency from parent to child is not clear in the Convention, and the Convention's monitoring committee, the Committee on the Rights of the Child, has only recently begun to look more closely at differentiating the particular rights of adolescent children from those of younger children.[37] Canon law differentiates the rights of children based on age and evolving capacity, and this is a debate it needs to continue to engage with. A future membership based on maintaining the practice of the automatic permanent enrolment of non-sentient infants is untenable in the long term.

Some people mistakenly believe that Confirmation provides the maturing child member with an opportunity for validation of his or her Church membership. It does not. In fact, the language used in the Rite of Confirmation calls on the child to confirm and "renew" his or her baptismal promises, completely disregarding the reality that over 80% of all Catholics never made such promises in the first place. Yet the sacrament of Confirmation could well provide an answer to how the Church can provide for the exercise of personal choice by its adolescent members. Bishop Brendan Leahy of the Diocese of Limerick, who is a civil lawyer as well as a canon lawyer and theologian, has opened a debate on the issue which, while not

....

36   United Nations Convention on the Rights of the Child, Article 14.2.

37   Committee on the Rights of the Child, General Comment no. 20.

couched in terms of children's rights, points in a very important direction. He asks:

> Are the boys and girls really aware what is going on? Are children opting or floating into Confirmation? [...] the child, instead of coming to know the Catholic faith as a new, challenging and meaningful horizon that can be opted into, often sees it as a pre-fabricated cultural package. [...] Might we not avail of the fact that Confirmation is still viewed as an important ritual and invite 16 year olds to celebrate the sacrament? [...] not all students would opt into it. But some/many would and at least it would come as an option with also a more living "adult" contact with the parish.[38]

As debate on international human rights and in particular the rights of the child develops, Church practice, teaching and law are going to come under closer scrutiny, whether by the UN monitoring agency the Committee on the Rights of the Child, or by an international or national court in response to questions from a citizen of a member state of the European Union or the Council of Europe, both of which have structures for the vindication of individual rights. The right to freedom of conscience, thought, belief and religion, including the freedom to change religion, is now binding on all member states of

38 Bishop of Limerick Brendan Leahy, Keynote address to Catholic Schools Week, Adare, Co. Limerick, Ireland, 21 January 2015. http://www.catholicireland.net/ bishop-catholic-schools-week/

the Council of Europe and the European Union.[39] The Catholic Church is not a member of the Council of Europe or the European Union, but many of its members live in countries that are, and many of the services the Church offers are performed in the jurisdictions of member states of both bodies.

The same is true of the Convention on the Rights of the Child. Every member of the United Nations is a State Party to the Convention, with the exception of the United States. It is the most ratified convention in the history of the United Nations. The Catholic Church, with its huge range of activities on behalf of children in many of the ratifying countries, is likely to have its services judged against the Convention's provisions by civil society child advocacy groups and even the courts in those other State Party jurisdictions in the coming years. Many of these jurisdictions also have forums for the vindication of their citizen's human rights. The Church has no such forum. We already know that it was not the Church itself but individuals, courts and secular civil society groups who exposed the awful narratives of Catholic institutional and clerical abuse of children. Failure to take the initiative and deal with its own internal problems has given the Church even greater problems and stresses, affecting the very fabric of the Church itself.

Engaging with the consequences of an out-dated conscription-based model of Church membership and converting it to a volunteer model could not only solve issues such as emptying churches and closed seminaries, but could also revitalise the

....

39 The rights set out in the UCHR and the E.U. Fundamental Charter of Rights apply to all.

Church, reenergising its catechesis by recalibrating its juridical relationship to baptised infants. Instead of becoming permanent members at birth who are from then on told what they must believe, the baptised infants could become quasi-catechumens, invited to transform an acknowledged provisional membership conferred at Baptism into a deep personal relationship with Christ and full membership of the Church when they are capable of doing so, if they wish to do so.

Church law does not currently recognise any explicit right of a baptised Catholic to make a conscientious clean break from the Church. It does not afford Church members recognition of their full human rights to freedom of expression, opinion, conscience and belief within the Church itself. It does not provide for a model of provisional membership at infant baptism, with full membership contingent upon full consent.

Yet in 1990, the Holy See became a State Party to the UN Convention on the Rights of the Child, and like all State Parties, it voluntarily committed itself to "respect the right of the child to freedom of thought, conscience and religion".[40] It has yet to reflect on what that means in practice for Church members.

Also awaiting deeper reflection are the words of the Second Vatican Council's Declaration on Religious Liberty, *Dignitatis Humanae*. It stated that that the human person has a right to religious freedom and that no one is to be forced to act in a

....

40   United Nations Convention on the Rights of the Child, Article 14.1.

manner contrary to his beliefs.[41] This view was summarised in the *Catechism of the Catholic Church* at paragraph 1782: "Man has the right to act in conscience and in freedom so as personally to make moral decisions. He must not be forced to act contrary to his conscience. Nor must he be prevented from acting according to his conscience, especially in religious matters." It was included in the 1983 *Code of Canon Law* which says that it is never "permitted to coerce persons to embrace the Catholic faith against their conscience".[42] But the devil is in the details for those who think these fine sentiments express the scope of freedoms enjoyed internally within the Church by its members. They do not. None of these quotes applies to members of the Church.

Instead they serve only to ensure that non-baptised persons or members of other Christian denominations are not forced to embrace the Catholic faith. 'Embracing' the faith is what the non-baptised do by becoming baptised, or what non-Catholic baptised Christians do by converting to Catholicism. 'Profess-

....

41 *Dignitatis Humanae*, Article 2: "The Vatican Council declares that the human person has a right to religious freedom. Freedom of this kind means that all men should be immune from coercion on the part of individuals, social groups and every human power so that, within due limits, nobody is forced to act against his convictions nor is anyone to be restrained from acting in accordance with his convictions in religious matters in private or in public, alone or in associations with others. The Council further declares that the right to religious freedom is based on the very dignity of the human person as known through the revealed word of God and by reason itself".

42 Code of Canon Law 1983, canon 748 §2.

ing' the faith is what baptised Catholics do by practising their faith. Church members (including those baptised as infants) are presumed to have embraced the faith at Baptism and are therefore obliged to profess the faith, which means honouring all the obligations that divine law and Church law imposes upon them, from confessing grave sins at the age of seven (with the use of reason) to facing punishment for the offences of heresy, apostasy and schism for challenging or rejecting Church teaching or authority.[43] The catechesis that infants receive post-baptism is informed by the assumption that they have already received the faith and accepted the obligations of membership of the Church. Their catechesis is categorical; it emphasises obligations already entered into, which require no personal ratification by baptised infants but which they are obliged by Church law to fulfil. The *Catechism of the Catholic Church* summarises their situation saying that Baptism as grace "is a grace of free, unmerited election and does not need ratification to become effective".[44] Here again we can see the failure to differentiate between the indelible spiritual effects of Baptism, which operate by grace, and the juridical effects that impose mandatory Church enrolment.

Pope Francis has written of the "offer of salvation",[45] which he notes is made to us by God[46] and "our acceptance of the

43 Cf. Code of Canon Law 1983, canon 748 §2.

44 Cf. Catechism of the Catholic Church, 1308.

45 Pope Francis, *Evangelii Gaudium*, 24 Nov. 2014, note 178, in *AAS* 105 (2013) 1019-1137.

46 Pope Francis, *Evangelii Gaudium*, 24 Nov. 2014, note 128, in AAS 105 (2013) 1019-1137.

message of salvation".[47] It sounds similar to the law of contract that I learnt in law school, which requires an offer by one side and acceptance by another. The civil law of contract in many jurisdictions, including Ireland, is generally sceptical of contracts entered into by adults for or on behalf of children that impose onerous obligations on those children. The more serious the contractual undertakings are, the more likely it is that civil law may insist on scrutinising of terms of the contract and rendering such a contract void when a child is older.[48]

The fundamental flaw in Church structure that endangers the future of the Church is that the offer of salvation described by Francis is made every day to thousands of babies at Baptism who have no idea of what the offer entails. They are presented for Baptism by parents and the offer Francis speaks of is accepted by the parents on the child's behalf, never by the child herself. It is done with the best of intentions, but the reality is it arguably offends a person's human rights to impose obligations as serious as those imposed by the Church at Baptism without giving the holder of those obligations a chance to later accept or reject them.

In 1995 the Committee on the Rights of the Child expressed its concern that the Holy See emphasised parental rights at the expense of children's rights, especially in the context of

47 Pope Francis, *Evangelii Gaudium*, 24 Nov. 2014, note 178, in *AAS* 105 (2013) 1019-1137.

48 Cf. United Kingdom, Infant Relief Act 1874. For a discussion of the civil law of contracts by minors see Law Reform Commission (Ireland), Report on minors' contracts.

the article 12, which asserts the religious liberty of the child[49]. Without citing any particular authority Mr Vincenzo Buonomo, a member of the Holy See delegation to the Committee, stated that recently there had been a certain evolution in the Church's thinking about the right to freedom of religion, especially where the child was concerned,[50] and that as far as the Church was concerned a parent could give his or her religion to a child but could not impose it.[51] Fr. Raymond Roch, also a member of the Holy See delegation, said that the Holy See's view of the interdependence between parental and children's rights was that parents ought to guide and advise children in a way that corresponded with the child's developmental capacity and conformed to the child's rights under the UNCRC. This line of debate, which never went beyond generalities, may well have led the CRC to believe erroneously that the Church gave its billion infant members the opportunity to validate their parents' choice or repudiate it when mature enough to do so. The Church does no such thing. But it would be good to know that it is, as Mr Buonomo asserted, evolving its thinking to bring it into line with the human right to full religious freedom. However, I have been unable to find any evidence that it is in fact evolving its thinking. In fact, the Church's recent embarrassingly contradictory engagement with the Commit-

49   CRC, Summary Record of 255th meeting held on 14 November 1995. Discussion of Holy See's Initial Report, 15.

50   CRC, Summary Record of 256th meeting held on 14 November 1995. Discussion of Holy See's Initial Report, 7.

51   CRC, Summary Record of 255th meeting held on 14 November 1995. Discussion of Holy See's Initial Report, 44.

tee on the Rights of the Child shows the opposite.[52] Having acknowledged that it freely ratified the UNCRC on behalf of two distinct entities, the Vatican City State and the Holy See, over twenty years after ratification the Holy See moved to inform the CRC (for the first time) that it was only obliged to implement the convention within the laws of the Vatican City State and not within the laws of the Church.[53] This view is strongly contradicted by the Committee on the Rights of the Child, which argues that the Holy See is a State party like all others and is obliged to implement the principles of the treaty within its own jurisdiction for the benefit of the children within that jurisdiction.

Ironically the Church insists that it is willing to and regularly docs advocate the principles sct out in the UNCRC to the world in general and to all people of good will. That outreach to the external world would be all the more credible if the Church was fully engaged in ensuring the internationally recognised human rights it says it supports are reflected in its teachings and laws.

The growing number of young people and adults exercising their human right to freely leave the Church in Ireland or to express opinions that contradict the Church could continue to grow. The massification of second and third level education,

52 Cf. Holy See, Comments on the Concluding Observations of the CRC on the Second Periodic Report on the UNCRC.

53 Cf. Holy See, Replies to the List of Issues raised by the CRC on the Second Periodic Report of the Holy See on the UNCRC; Comments on the Concluding Observations of the CRC on the Second Periodic Report on the UNCRC.

which is often done with the help of the religious orders and the Church, is creating highly educated young adults well able to interrogate and test Church teaching in ways the past made too difficult. The Church is at a crossroads. It has a choice. It can turn this creeping existential threat into a disaster by ignoring it, or it can turn it into a spring tide by dealing with it. It cannot afford the luxury of presuming that because of its simple numerical strength, it has time on its side.

Leabharlanna Poiblí Chathair Baile Átha Cliath
Dublin City Public Libraries